SONORAN
DESERT

Southwest Parks and Monuments Association

Tucson, Arizona

Great Basin

Mojave Desert

Sonoran Desert

Chihuahuan Desert

Dawn in the Desert

At sunrise, soft peach-colored light paints the eastern horizon. A melodic chorus of mourning doves, curve-billed thrashers, and Gambel's quail melts into the air, while a raucous cactus wren rat-a-tat-tats from a spiny cholla. A downy cottontail rabbit speeds off to a sheltering shrub. Ocotillos, abloom with flame-tipped branches, spice the tawny slopes.

Dawn in the Sonoran Desert is a time to cherish. The stillness and inviting coolness rouse all inhabitants to activity. It's the time to savor the qualities of this amazing desert, to saunter down a dry wash, to see hummingbirds, watch lizards, and admire wildflowers. It's the time for everything and everyone to move, to hunt, to sing. For even in early April, it won't be long before the sullen heat bears down like a sledgehammer, driving most living things to seek shade for the day.

Organic Pipe Cactus
National Monument,
Arizona

The Sonoran is one of four major deserts of North America, along with the Mojave, Chihuahuan, and Great Basin. As with all the deserts, the Sonoran is defined generally by the circumstance of little rainfall that arrives unpredictably. Dry winds suck up what moisture does fall, humidity is low, and direct, unfiltered sunlight sears the land. Climate—primarily seasonal heating of the earth's surface and global wind patterns that generate strong shifts in storm tracks—dictates the locations of the deserts. They are held up by the bookends of the Sierra Nevada on the west and the Rocky Mountains and Sierra Madre on the east, and they share a geological heritage and common landforms.

Desert cottontails live in the lower portions of the Sonoran Desert, often in brushy areas.

The purple-tinged pads of the Santa Rita prickly pear cactus are as lovely as the yellow blossoms.

Thanks to its particular geographic location, the Sonoran Desert enjoys two seasons of rainfall. Rains in both summer and winter define this desert and nourish its larger trees and shrubs, earning it the description of "arboreal" desert.

In fact, the Sonoran almost defies the word "desert." Even in drought, its overall sense is lavish greenness. The best way to tell you're in the Sonoran Desert is by the presence of trees—mesquites, paloverdes, ironwoods—and the signature saguaro cactus that reaches tree size. The climatic—and hence biological—origins of this desert are tropical and subtropical, which also helps explain its unique "feel."

The cactus wren, Arizona's state bird, builds its nest among spiny cactus.

Boundaries

Nearly two-thirds of the Sonoran Desert's 120,000 square miles lie in the namesake state in Mexico. In the United States it covers southeast California and southern Arizona. Elevations range from sea level to about 3,000 to 4,000 feet. The upland portion, in central and southern Arizona, is blessed by up to a foot of rain a year and harbors the saguaro-paloverde community. The Colorado Desert subdivision—the largest and hottest—is the low-elevation portion from Yuma, Arizona, westward to El Centro, California. Rainfall in this portion can be a scant two inches a year, supporting a simple plant community consisting mostly of two shrubs—creosote bush and white bursage.

The boundaries of the Sonoran Desert are sharpest near the higher mountains on the northeast edge, but they tend to blur in the northwest corner around Needles, California, where the Sonoran grades into the neighboring Mojave Desert. The Sonoran Desert's southwest edge runs through the middle of Joshua Tree National Park. In the far southeast corner of Arizona, the San Pedro River marks the farthest eastern limits of the saguaro cactus, and the Sonoran Desert.

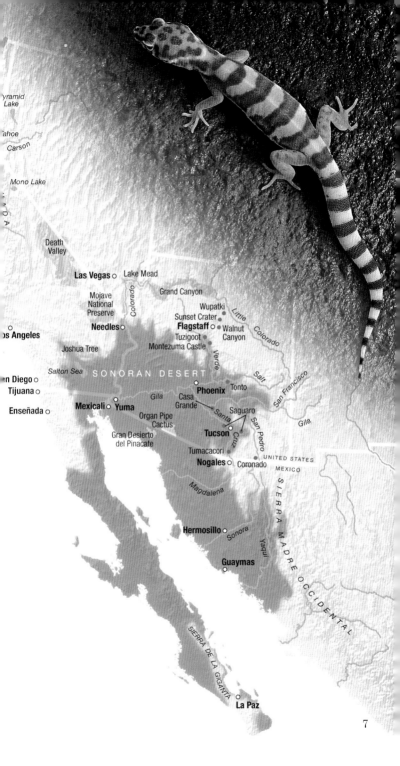

yramid
Lake

ahoe

Carson

Mono Lake

Death
Valley

Las Vegas ○ Lake Mead

Mojave
National
Preserve

Colorado

Grand Canyon

Wupatki
Sunset Crater
Flagstaff ○ Walnut
Canyon

Little

Colorado

Needles ○

os Angeles

Joshua Tree

Tuzigoot
Montezuma Castle

Verde

S O N O R A N   D E S E R T

Salt

San Francisco

Salton Sea

n Diego ○
Tijuana ○

Phoenix

Tonto

Enseñada ○

Mexicali ○ Yuma

Gila

Casa
Grande

Organ Pipe
Cactus

Santa

Saguaro

San Pedro

Gila

Gran Desierto
del Pinacate

Tucson

Cruz

Tumacacori

Nogales ○ Coronado

UNITED STATES

MEXICO

Magdalena

SIERRA MADRE OCCIDENTAL

Hermosillo ○ Sonora

Guaymas

Yaqui

SIERRA DE LA GIGANTA

La Paz

7

Desert Mountains

Mountain ranges both abrupt and gentle punctuate the edge and dot the interior of the Sonoran Desert. Many of these ranges, such as the Tucson Mountains in Saguaro National Park, are the result of explosive volcanism. About 70 million years ago, eruptions occurred on the Santa Catalina Mountains that preside over the city of Tucson to the north. The volcano collapsed in on itself and created a caldera. During a period of extension 30 million to 17 million years ago, the Tucson Mountains slid off the Catalinas and settled at their present westward location.

The Basin and Range province, to which the Sonoran Desert belongs, was born during that period of extension. The mountains reared up as blocks along faults, while the valleys between them dropped down. Most of the mountains of the Sonoran Desert march to the same tune—trending northwest-southeast, separated by broad valleys.

Tucson Mountains,
Arizona

The Growler, Ajo, Sand Tanks, Maricopas, and many other ranges appear like islands afloat within the surrounding desert. The mountains' size, elevation, orientation, and rock types give rise to innumerable "micro" environments, lending immense diversity to the desert. Most are low enough that they are still clothed in desert plants. But a few, such as the Santa Ritas and the Catalinas, rise to more than 9,000 feet, high enough to support forests of oak, juniper, and pine. Slope orientation is extremely important. Cooler, wetter north-facing slopes are more heavily vegetated, while hotter, drier south-facing slopes support dryland species. Rock types of differing texture and chemistry shape plant life. Ocotillo, for example, seem to prefer limestones, while creosote bush can survive in the dense clay soils of the valleys.

The mountains of the Sonoran Desert ease into foothills, which splay at their bases into graceful bajadas (pronounced ba-HAH-dah). These cone-shaped features are collections of sand, silt, and boulders borne by water down the steep mountain slopes. As a bajada forms, the sediments are "sorted" into coarser rocks at the top, grading into finer ones at the base. A trip around the Bajada Loop Drive in Saguaro National Park West provides a good close-up view of this classic desert landform.

Native fan palms

Groves of graceful California fan palms, Washingtonia filifera, are found in a few isolated spots in the Kofa Mountains in southwest Arizona and in Joshua Tree National Park as well. These native palms are nourished by water that rises at springs, often along fault lines. The places where they are found are true oases in the desert. Occasionally, beneath the shade of these tall trees grow hanging gardens of orchids and maidenhair ferns. Their "skirts" of dead palm fronds alive with the rustlings of birds. Native Americans used them for shelter, basketry, and hats. The wood and the fruit of the palm were put to use too.

Bajadas spill out into the broad valleys that are filled thousands of feet deep with alluvium, the mountains literally burying themselves in their own debris. Washes scratch across the land, dry except when summer rainstorms fill them bank-full. A few rivers still flow—the Colorado, which marks the border between Arizona and California, and the San Pedro. Others, such as the Santa Cruz, Salt, and Gila Rivers, run only during big floods.

Soils form with agonizing slowness in the desert. They contain precious little organic material, but an abundance of calcium and salts. What soil does collect is readily washed or blown away, unless armored by a mosaic of small stones called desert pavement.

Sabino Canyon

The beautiful waters of Sabino Creek tumble down Sabino Canyon on the south face of the Santa Catalina Mountains. The sycamore-lined stream, flowing year-round beside saguaro-studded hillsides, is a microenvironment for animals that depend on water—belted kingfishers, black-necked garter snakes, spadefoot toads, and raccoons.

Fringe-toed lizard

Sandy areas of the Sonoran Desert are the places to find the fringe-toed lizard. The fringes are a comb of pointed scales on the edge of its toes that let this lizard "swim" into sand to avoid predators and scorching temperatures. But that's not all. It also comes equipped with fringed eyelids and earflaps that help keep out grit, and the lizard's light tan body blends beautifully with the sand.

Great sloping bajadas spill off mountains in the Sonoran Desert, like these in the Galiuro Mountains of Arizona.

Though the popular image of desert is a vast sea of sand, the Sonoran Desert within the United States possesses only one large body of sand—the Algodones Dunes. The Algodones Dunes were once the beach sands of Lake Cahuilla, the ice-age predecessor of the Salton Sea. Northwesterly winds blew the sands to the east where they settled into elegant high dunes along the lower end of the Colorado River. Though their source material is gone now, the Algodones Dunes are still moving. Following especially good winter rains, the rippling dunes erupt in a riot of flowers. Yellow evening primroses, white desert lilies, and pink sand verbenas grace them, anchored by long stems and roots that tap moisture deep in the sand.

San Pedro River

The San Pedro River marks the eastern boundary of the Sonoran Desert. The San Pedro flows north out of Mexico into southeast Arizona, carrying water year-round and bounded by a rare mesquite-cottonwood-willow forest. Some 350 species of birds, including yellow-billed cuckoos, gray hawks, and green kingfishers, flock to its banks. Several million migrating songbirds pass through this corridor annually. At least eight species of mammals, forty species of amphibians and reptiles, and two native species of fish live in this precious riparian area. The San Pedro's value has been recognized by designation as a Riparian National Conservation Area.

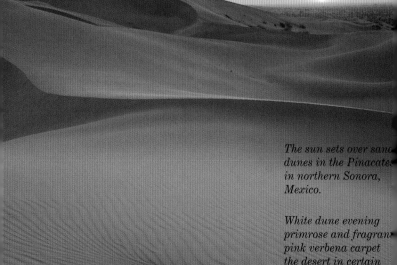

The sun sets over sand dunes in the Pinacate in northern Sonora, Mexico.

White dune evening primrose and fragrant pink verbena carpet the desert in certain years.

Seasons in the Desert

The upland portion of the Sonoran Desert boasts not four, but five, seasons: spring, foresummer, summer monsoon, after summer, and winter. Springtime, from mid-February through April, is warm and dry. Paloverdes along the washes and in the foothills are covered with yellow blooms in April, like big lemon drops. Ocotillo sprout leaves and flowers. Annuals such as poppies, phacelias, lupines, and owl's clover splash the ground in bright colors if winter rains have been good. Birds breed and nest.

May and June, called foresummer, are two months of desiccating heat and dryness. Despite the conditions, most animals try to reproduce during this season. Among them are Gila monsters, breeding and then laying eggs underground that must overwinter before hatching.

Also in May and June, the steadfast saguaros bear flowers. They presage the next season, the one that marks the real New Year in the Sonoran Desert, the summer monsoon. Usually beginning by early July, these vigorous afternoon storms are greeted with wild delight. Lightning tongues to the ground, and brief but torrential rains pelt the earth. In a matter of hours, the miracle of water brings the desert to life. Insects hatch, toads and tree frogs emerge, hummingbirds

16

Superstition
Mountains, Arizona

Snowmelt roars down Sabino Creek in the Santa Catalina Mountains north of Tucson.

The Ajo, or desert, lily graces the desert with glorious blooms in spring.

Succulent fruits of organ pipe cactus have fed animals and people in the desert for millennia.

18

A monsoon gathers at sunrise over the Kofa National Wildlife Refuge in south-western Arizona.

Backlit silvery spines of teddy bear cholla gleam on desert hillsides.

A summer flash flood funnels down a normally dry creek bed in Organ Pipe Cactus National Monument.

19

hover at nectar-filled flowers, and the fruits of the saguaro ripen into succulent red morsels.

Desert dwellers anxiously wait to hear National Weather Service meteorologists pronounce the arrival of the monsoon season. To make it official, the daily dew point in Tucson must reach 54 degrees or more three days in a row. The average start date is July 5, but monsoon conditions have begun as early as June 19 and as late as July 25. Southerly winds usher in moisture from the Gulf of California and the Gulf of Mexico, and by the time the monsoon season ends, usually in mid-September, Tucson may have received an average of five and half inches of rain.

Following the monsoon excitement, aftersummer sets in. This is autumn in the Sonoran Desert, though temperatures stay high through September. By October and November most hummingbirds, turkey vultures, flycatchers, and orioles have left, and the heat finally starts to wane.

As most "snowbirds" well know, winter in the Sonoran Desert is short but sweet. December and January mark the second rainy season, this one gentler than the dramatic summer downpours. Snows sometimes whiten the surrounding mountains and occasionally dust the valleys, if only for a day. The length of frost and freezes is critical to desert plants, most of which are by their nature intolerant of cold.

Black-chinned hummingbird

A host of hummingbirds zip through the air in summer. Among the most common in the Sonoran Desert is the black-chinned hummingbird. A metallic green breast and violet band around their black throat mark the males. These and most other hummingbirds fuel their feverish metabolism with the sugary nectar of flowers, especially red, tube-shaped blossoms. While engaged in nectar sipping, the birds also gather pollen and transfer it to other plants. Hummingbirds help pollinate at least fifty species of flowers in Arizona alone.

Gila monsters

Gila monsters spend most of their days basking in the sun near rocky retreats. Or they loll in cool underground burrows, coming out in early morning and evening to forage for food. These are exquisite lizards, with black and coral beaded skin. And they are fearsome in size—at up to two feet long, Gila monsters are the largest lizards in the United States. They are one of two venomous lizards in the world. The other is a similar looking relative, the Mexican beaded lizard.

Great Vegetable Spirits

No other plant better defines the Sonoran Desert than the saguaro cactus. This desert is the only place in the world where saguaros grow. When explorer William Hornaday first saw the "giant cactus" around Tucson, Arizona, in 1907, he exclaimed: "It is this strange plant, more than any other...that most strongly impresses upon the mind of the traveler the fact that *this is another world*!" Some of the finest stands of saguaros are preserved in the more than 93,000 acres of Saguaro National Park, on both the east and west sides of Tucson.

Stoic saguaros march up the rocky slopes and glow like candelabras in the late afternoon light. It's hard to imagine that each one started as a tiny black seed the size of a drop of ink. When mature, saguaros can reach more than fifty feet in height and weigh several tons. Slow-growing, the mightiest patriarchs may be a couple of centuries old. A woody skeleton supports the saguaro, and with the pleated green exterior tissue the plant can expand and contract like an accordion as water supplies warrant. Shallow, wide-spreading roots help saguaros rehydrate in a hurry, whenever moisture is available.

Saguaro National
Park, Arizona

Though a single saguaro may produce tens of millions of seeds in a lifetime, only a few are chosen to become seedlings. After germinating in warm summer rains, vulnerable seedlings will need the shelter of a "nurse" shrub or tree and will need to miss the jaws of hungry ants or rodents. A ten-year-old saguaro can be measured in inches; by fifty years it may be six or seven feet tall. In the next twenty-five years the plants reach reproductive age and begin to sprout arms, or branches. Certain saguaros shoot out several arms, some twisting and bending into fabulous contortionist poses, while old ones may not have one arm. Big white flowers usually open in April and early May, circling the tops of the branches like garlands. Each flower remains open for only twenty-four hours, and because not all the flowers open on the same day, the bloom continues for some time. By June, though, the flowers have transformed into the seed-filled fruits that split open like red stars pinned to the branches.

Saguaros grow farther north than any other columnar cacti, yet like their kin they are critically sensitive to freezing temperatures, which is why they fare best on warmer, south-facing slopes of the bajadas. As author David Lazaroff observes, the distribution of saguaros creates a "map of winter sunshine." Seedlings on north-facing slopes don't get as much sunshine on winter days and are

The ripening of saguaro cactus fruit in summer months marks the beginning of the New Year among native people of the Sonoran Desert.

vulnerable to freezes and later to drought. Those on south-facing slopes enjoy longer hours of sun and warmth; morning sunlight, especially, may be a key to saguaro growth.

Each saguaro is an ecosystem unto itself, and members of this tightly entwined community may be seen from the Cactus Forest Trail in Saguaro National Park East. The flowers are platforms for bees, bats, and doves divining for nectar and pollen; coyotes and foxes relish the juicy fruits that fall to the ground; and Gila woodpeckers and gilded flickers excavate nest sites in the fleshy green trunks. When the woodpeckers are done with them, kestrels, warblers, cactus wrens, and kingbirds vie for this valuable real estate. Sparrow-sized elf owls, the smallest owls in North America, use the hollow holes too, their beady yellow eyes staring out from these deliciously cool summer homes. Even in decay, a saguaro supports life. Fruit flies, cactus flies, and hover flies feed, mate, and lay eggs among the decaying tissues.

Where saguaros grow, they are often found in association with foothill paloverdes. The name paloverde, Spanish for "green stick," gives a clue to its survival tactics. The tree saves water by discarding its tiny leaves, and even twigs and branches, during dry times; but photosynthesis continues through the green bark. These are slow-growing, long-lived trees, some

A great horned owl nestling finds shelter in the crook of saguaro branches.

Contorted spiny ribs reveal the wooden skeleton that supported a giant saguaro cactus.

reaching a century or more in age. Paloverdes bloom with pale yellow flowers as spring draws to a close in the desert.

Paloverdes provide insects and nest sites for verdins and other desert birds. Birds roosting in the trees at night may void the saguaro seeds they ate and cannot digest, hence one reason saguaros and paloverdes grow together. Foothill paloverdes also require the same rocky, well-drained soils and warmer south-facing slopes that saguaros do.

Paloverdes play host to a mean-looking black and orange wasp called a tarantula hawk. Biologist John Alcock tells how an individual male tarantula hawk will commandeer a paloverde in the spring, holding competitors at bay as it tries to attract females. Later, when the tree's seeds fall to the ground, pocket mice and packrats devour them. These rodents cache some seeds in the ground, relocating them later by smell. Those they don't find may germinate after rains and become young paloverdes.

While the saguaro is the best known cactus of the Sonoran Desert, another columnar cactus shares the spotlight. It is the organ pipe cactus, which just barely inches over the Mexican border into the United States. This is the plant that led to establishment of Organ Pipe Cactus National Monument in far southern

Bats

Long-nosed bats, denizens of desert nights, migrate north from Mexico as the saguaro and other columnar cacti bloom. Attracted by the flowers' musky odor, the bats emerge from roosts after sunset and pay visits to the open flowers, dipping their long tongues in to extract nectar, their source of liquid. Once the cactus bloom is over, the bats continue on the "nectar trail" to agaves, whose flowering peaks in July and early August. Long-nosed bats are important pollinators of these plants, but birds, bees, and other insects help too.

Packrat middens

A prickly, impenetrable mass of sticks and spiny cactus stems form the armored domicile of a packrat, a rodent that builds large middens of plant material it finds nearby, and anything else the animal can haul in. Because generations of packrats use the same spot year after year, the middens are gold mines for paleontologists who analyze the contents for clues to past environments. Due to evidence from middens, we now know the Sonoran Desert is a recent environment— today's plant communities developed only over the last 4,000 to 8,000 years, since the end of the last ice age.

Arizona. A trip around Puerto Blanco Drive in the park takes visitors past impressive stands of organ pipe cacti and through the heart of the Sonoran Desert.

Where saguaros and organ pipes grow side by side, their differences are apparent. Not as large or massive as a saguaro, an organ pipe cactus has multiple green stems rising gracefully from the base of the plant, like the pipes on an organ. Each slender stem is lined with vertical rows of dark spines. Like the saguaro, organ pipe cacti are frost-sensitive and flourish on south-facing slopes. They also produce nocturnal white flowers and delectable fruits coveted by wildlife.

Another cactus within Organ Pipe Cactus National Monument is an uncommon one. The acuña cactus, highly specific in its habitat (only loose, chipped granite on hilltops will do), is likely rare by nature. Acuña cacti have become even harder to find because something, possibly a washout or digging animals, has regularly uprooted many specimens on a plot where biologists have been counting and tagging them for years. Their search for the minute seedlings is a tedious task—down on hands and knees looking "for snowflakes on stones," as one biologist puts it. The discovery of a tiny seedling is cause for celebration. Reproduction has become so infrequent among the acuña that seeds are not plentiful. Those that are produced are usually harvested wholesale by ants.

Organ Pipe Cactus
National Monument,
Arizona

While the saguaro and other pretty-blooming cacti tend to get the glory, another plant probably deserves more respect, if only for sheer abundance and fortitude. It's the creosote bush, the shrub that grows over millions of acres in the valleys of the Sonoran Desert. In fact, creosote bush covers about 70 percent of the total acreage in all three of the warm deserts—the Sonoran, Mojave, and Chihuahuan. It is, in the words of desertologist Edmund Jaeger, "that remarkable plant which marks better than any other the domain of the real American desert."

Creosote bushes cast an overall olive color to the brown-tan landscape. Their limber branches wave pleasingly in the wind, and well-watered plants are covered with lemony yellow flowers that become furry round seeds. There's only one species of creosote bush in this country—*Larrea tridentata*—the species name alluding to the three-toothed leaf. Unlike cacti, many of which require rocky habitat that gives up more moisture to their roots, creosote bush germinates and thrives in the finer-grained valley soils.

Finding sparse food and cover, few birds live year-round in the creosote bush flats. Only one, the black-throated sparrow, is commonly seen. But other animals find the shrubs good habitat. Soft mounds of dirt at the base of creosote bushes are pockmarked with holes made by mice, kangaroo rats, and other small rodents.

Creosote bush flats

Kangaroo rat

Small, tawny-colored rodents called kangaroo rats bounce across roads at night in the desert. They are propelled by powerful hind legs, and possess gorgeous long tails that work like rudders K-rats, as they're fondly called, are famous for their capacity to go without free water. They obtain all the moisture they need from seeds, which they stash in their cheek pouches and take back to their burrows for later consumption. Supremely adapted to conserve water, kangaroo rats do not perspire, they produce concentrated urine, and they are nocturnal in habit.

Phainopeplas

Mesquite trees line desert washes, their lacy leaves casting delicious shade. Often perched conspicuously in the topmost branches is a glossy black bird with a jaunty crest, the phainopepla. The males breed with the less showy females once in early spring in the desert lowlands, then head for northern woodlands where they breed again in May and June. Phainopeplas return to the desert in the fall, where they indulge in one of their favorite foods, the berries of desert mistletoe. The sticky seeds pass through the birds' digestive systems, landing on other mesquites and thus helping spread the parasitic mistletoe.

These burrows, often twenty degrees cooler than the ground surface, make fine places to hide out during the heat of the day. Creosote bushes also host a large number of insects—grasshoppers, bagworms, lac insects, carpenter bees, as well as many different kinds of galls, growths on the stems that house insect larvae.

In Mexico creosote bush is called *el gobernador*, the governor, for its predominance and its ability to keep other plants out by "governing" its territory. It does this because it emits toxins that exclude plants from growing nearby that would compete with it for water. In obvious reference to the scent, creosote bush is called *hediondilla*, or little stinker.

Creosote bush is a survivor. The sticky, resinous leaves persist when everything else in the desert has gone into a death-watch during stressful dry times. The unpalatable resins deter browsers, and chemical compounds in those resins are being investigated as a food preservative and as a curative for arthritis and bronchial problems among others. A botanist traveling through the Sonoran Desert in the nineteenth century also observed local people chewing the plant to relieve thirst. When it rains the air is permeated with the distinct aroma of damp creosote, so heady that it induces serious nostalgia in desert dwellers. Some people have even been known to hang creosote branches in their showers as a reminder.

Jojoba

On rock and gravel slopes a medium-sized shrub with oval, blue-green leaves stands out among the other smaller-leaved shrubs. It is jojoba (pronounced ho-HO-ba), which grows only in the Sonoran Desert. The fruit, which resembles an acorn, gives the plant alternate names of goat-nut and coffeeberry. The rich waxy oil of the nuts serves as a substitute for sperm whale oil in cosmetics, lubricants, and car waxes.

Ironwood

Along larger drainages grow ironwood trees, *Olneya tesota*, or often just *tesota*, whose distribution very nearly describes the bounds of the Sonoran Desert. Intolerant of cold, ironwoods usually grow at low, warm elevations. A member of the legume, or pea, family, this large tree has filigree leaves and wood so dense it sinks in water. Ironwood often grows with mesquite, and when ironwood bursts into bloom, the bounteous bluish-purple flowers are unmistakable. Then the trees buzz with digger bees looking for pollen and nectar. Rock squirrels invade to harvest the seeds. After the dried pods fall, the ground beneath the trees fairly crackles as packrats, peccaries, and pocket mice hull the pods to remove the seeds.

Thanks to Saturday morning cartoons, nearly everyone recognizes roadrunners. They dash across desert roads, tails held high, necks stuck out—you can almost hear them go beep-beep. But these residents of the Sonoran Desert are more than caricatures. Greater roadrunners, as they are more properly known, are ground dwellers. Rarely do they fly. They streak by, nabbing insects, scorpions, lizards, snakes, and small birds. After catching a lizard or a snake, these birds have been known to bat it on a rock before swallowing it.

Coyote

The cosmopolitan coyote is common in the Sonoran Desert. This wary-eyed traveler may be seen trotting across the road into the bushes. It's called the "song dog" for a complex repertoire of vocalizations. Campers in the desert can expect to be treated to a serenade on almost any full-moon night. Canis latrans is about the size of a small German shepherd; the thick fur is grizzled gray to tan. Omnivorous coyotes will eat nearly anything, animal or vegetable.

A smaller shrub with grayish-green leaves and purple flowers, white bursage, is the creosote's constant companion. Found often beneath bursage is the parasitic broomrape, a fleshy, colorless herb that attaches to the roots and obtains nutrients. Among other shrubs is the lovely fairy duster, which fans out feathery pink plumes in spring; and brittlebush, with dusty-gray leaves, mounded with flamboyant yellow, daisy-like flowers. When broken, the brittle branches exude a fragrant sap once used by priests as incense. *Incienso* is the Spanish name for this common plant.

The usually dry washes that slash down the bajada are natural corridors for animals. They are good places to spy the collared peccary, or javelina. These pig-like animals snuffle along searching out tubers to eat. With special physiological adaptations, they can survive on prickly pear pads when times get hard. Lots of different kinds of lizards are about when nothing else seems to be moving. Large collared lizards, with dark bands around their necks, are especially striking. They perch on rocks, glaring with a prehistoric look, doing "pushups" in a display of territoriality or just to keep their bodies cool.

The Desert as Home

A picture of the earliest human presence in the Sonoran Desert can be painted with only the broadest brush. As true desert conditions gained a grip, beginning about 8,000 years ago, the big game and those who hunted them were gone. Water sources grew scarcer, and the so-called Archaic people turned to smaller animals and learned to harvest hundreds of edible desert plants.

A watershed change came about in the Sonoran Desert when corn was introduced, and people settled in villages, tending the crops and praying for rain. Along the lower Colorado River valley, the Patayan and Hakataya cultivated small garden plots along the river and camped in the desert and mountains. Better known are their neighbors to the east, the Hohokam, who emerged as a distinct culture in the Sonoran Desert around A.D. 400.

The Hohokam lived in simple pole and mud pithouses, but they built a few multistory "great houses" such as the famed Casa Grande south of Phoenix, along with intriguing platform mounds and ballcourts. Most of all, the Hohokam were known for their irrigation works.

The Casa Grande, built by the Hohokam near the Gila River in the early 1300s, is one of only three such structures known.

Petroglyphs were pecked onto the faces of boulders by early inhabitants of the Sonoran Desert. The meaning of the art remains a mystery.

Hohokam projectile points, used as the tips of arrows, were carefully chipped of durable stone.

They dug hundreds of miles of canals in the hard-packed soil of the Salt and Gila River valleys around present-day Phoenix, and south in the Tucson Basin. They diverted water through an elaborate system of ditches to fields of corn, beans, squash, cotton, and tobacco.

After many long and productive centuries, the Hohokam culture collapsed around A.D. 1400 to 1450. Their demise remains a mystery, but it may be that their far-reaching irrigation systems failed, paradoxically due to floods rather than drought.

The probable descendants of the Hohokam are the O'odham. The O'odham have lived lives supremely adapted to their desert environment. To survive in the harshest territory, some remained mobile, while others practiced a range of farming techniques to assure success. They knew where all the water sources were, and for them the desert was a pantry filled with wild plants that could be eaten or used as medicine.

The word *O'odham* is both the name for the people and sometimes for the saguaro cactus, which to them embodies human qualities. Their New Year begins in June, the seed blackening time, when the saguaro fruits ripen, ready for harvest. From the juice of the fruit the O'odham make a fermented ceremonial drink, as part of an old ritual of calling down the rain to water their crops.

Tohono O'odham dwellings are called "ki's."

O'odham women at the turn of the twentieth century were known for their intricately designed baskets.

Souls and Silver

Spaniards, who arrived in the Sonoran Desert in 1540, were the first to encounter the O'odham. The upper Sonoran Desert became known as Pimería Alta, a land valued by the Spaniards not for its wondrous native plants, but for its mineral wealth and wayward souls waiting for salvation. In 1687 Jesuit priest Eusebio Kino crossed north over the "rim of Christendom," as historian Herbert Bolton called it. Traveling thousands of miles on horseback through Pimería Alta, Father Kino established churches and missions. As a result of his travels, geographic knowledge of the Sonoran Desert was greatly enhanced, for he documented the true courses of the major rivers and the exact location of the head of the Gulf of California. As Father Charles Polzer observed, Kino realized that in the arid desert "Life is more meaningful where life seems not to be."

Mexico, then the United States, eventually gained control of the desert and tried to ignore or conquer it. Glittering gold, silver, and copper caught people's eyes. Some 20,000 thirsty forty-niners threaded their way across southern Arizona's desert, bound for California in 1849 and 1850. They learned the realities of the desert the hard way. Along with mining, Hispanics and Anglos built an economy on the desert frontier by hauling

freight, milling flour, and raising cattle, finding a ready buyer among the Army posts set up to subdue the Indians.

The rich layers of human history in the Sonoran Desert are revealed in a little patch of greenery down on the border in Organ Pipe Cactus National Monument. It is Quitobaquito Springs, a name translated to "wet place where a little house is." Here warm springs seep down the slopes of the Puerto Blanco Mountains and feed a shallow pond. Bunches of saltgrass and fragrant yerba mansa grow around the spring itself. Tall bulrush rim the pond, and a few willows, condalia, wolfberry, and mesquite add to the verdant scene.

Wherever water appears in the desert, animals are sure to follow. Green herons, American coots, and warblers find hospitable habitat at Quitobaquito. Sonoran mud turtles bask in the sun on logs. Mountain lions drag mule deer to pond's edge and dine on them over several weeks.

For people, Quitobaquito has been a crossroads in the desert for thousands of years. Native Americans set up temporary camps where they ground mesquite beans, skinned game, roasted agave, and planted corn. An old salt trail passed here, leading to the Gulf of California where the Hohokam journeyed for salt and shells, coveted trade items. The Hia-Ced O'odham, the Sand People, lived at Quitobaquito and still come back for special ceremonies. To them it was *A'al Waipia*, Little Wells.

Padre Kino knew Quitobaquito too. Through the years O'odham, Mexicans, and Americans built a small settlement of adobe houses, a store, and a corral, and channeled the water to fields and orchards of pomegranates and fig trees.

Around 1910, desert explorer Karl Lumholtz found the crystal clear water most refreshing after three weeks of drinking brackish liquids. And, he divulged, it provided his "first real wash" in nine days.

By the time Lumholtz toured the desert at the dawn of the twentieth century, many American Indians had been placed on reservations, the Southern Pacific Railroad had laid track eastward across the desert, and homesteaders flowed in and staked their claims.

Tucson and Phoenix were still dusty desert towns, but all that would change as more people sought out the desert for its healthful dry air and for scientific exploration. The Carnegie Institution opened a laboratory on Tumamoc Hill above Tucson in 1902. Among the workers there was plant ecologist Forrest Shreve, whose forty years of research on the plant life of the Sonoran Desert remains a guiding light for scientists today.

The Hia-Ced O'odham call Quitobaquito Aial Waipia.

Desert pupfish

In springtime, the male pupfish at Quitobaquito Springs are as blue as the desert sky. This is their color during breeding season, when they spread their fins and dart through the water in attempts to attract receptive females and deter the advances of other males into their territories. These diminutive fish, only about two inches long, have to get in a lot of living in their two-year life spans. Amazingly adaptable creatures, pupfish can survive in warm, often salty, water most fish could not tolerate.

Diamondback rattlesnake

The western diamondback rattlesnake is one of several species of rattlesnakes in the Sonoran Desert. Three to four feet long, with a big head and heavy body, this is the largest rattler in the West. Though not especially aggressive, when frightened or cornered a diamondback will coil, rattle its tail, and strike with fangs that inject venom contained in glands. The bite can be fatal. This snake is fairly common and widely distributed, from sea level to 7,000 feet, from rocky canyons up into the foothills. They may be out sunning themselves on a warm spring day and searching for food on summer nights.

To Shreve, summer storms in the Sonoran Desert were a miracle. Their arrival marked the "most important biological episode of the year." In a few hours, plants and animals awake from dormancy. "In a single stroke," Shreve wrote, "the country is transformed from desert to tropics."

The first rains of the year are like sunrise in the desert, awakening and bringing new beginnings. And like the early mornings, the rains mark the time when life revives, when all things once again move and hunt and sing.

Saguaro National Park, Arizona